Holin

Saint Bonaventure

Translated by
Laurence Costello O.F.M.

Holiness of Life

Saint Bonaventure

Translated by
Laurence Costello O.F.M.

Edited and Re-typeset by
Paul A. Böer, Sr.

VERITATIS SPLENDOR PUBLICATIONS
et cognoscetis veritatem et veritas liberabit vos (Jn 8:32)

MMXV

Cover art:
HERRERA, Francisco de, the Elder
St Bonaventure Enters the Franciscan Order
1628
Oil on canvas, 231 x 215 cm
Museo del Prado, Madrid

Excerpted from
Holiness of Life. St. Bonaventure. Tr. Laurence Costello, OFM (US: B. Herder Book Company, 1923).

Retypeset and republished in 2015 by Veritatis Splendor Publications.

Veritatis.splendor.publication@gmail.com

AD MAJOREM DEI GLORIAM

Table of Contents

Holiness of Life

Saint Bonaventure

Translated by
Laurence Costello O.F.M.

1923 by B. Herder Book Company, US.

Saint Bonaventure's Holiness of Life (De perfectione vitæ ad sorores.)

REFACE

lessed is the man whom Thou shalt instruct, O Lord, and shalt ach out of Thy Law" (Ps. xciii, 12.) I hold that only the man ught by the Holy Spirit and imbued with His blessed unction is be considered wise. The Prophet David lays down the same inciple; he alone is really happy and wise whose mind the ord has made learned in the Law. "The Law of God," David otes elsewhere (Ps. xviii, 8), is the only law "without fault" and reproachable. It alone has the secret of "converting souls" to e way of salvation. To read the Law does not suffice. We only iscover its wealth of meaning and reap the fruits of its profound arning through devout and affectionate meditation.

onscientiously, "in Spirit and in truth" (1 Thess. i, 5.), are we to eek this meaning. We must beg the Holy Spirit, with ardent nging, to give us these fruits. The Holy Ghost alone knows ow to bring to light the sweetness hidden away under the gged exterior of the words of the Law. We must go to the Holy host for interior guidance.

he Law of the Lord teaches us the way to live, what is to be one, avoided, believed, prayed for, longed for and feared. It aches how to live the blameless and spotless life, how to keep ne's promises, and how to be sincerely contrite for one's ilings. The Law of the Lord teaches contempt for earthly things nd a loathing for all things of the flesh. Finally, it explains how ith our whole heart, whole soul, and whole mind we are to be onverted to Jesus Christ (Matt, xxii, 37.)

ompared with the doctrine of God's Law, worldly wisdom is ain and foolish. "As long as a man does not fear or love God, o matter how great his reputation for wisdom may be," says St. ernard, "I shall never consider him wise" (S. Bern. Serm. 73 de iversis.) I would remind you that many forget what they hear, ut these are not numbered among the wise. The truly wise man acts, and does zealously what the Law prescribes. The doer is the wise and the happy man. “Blessed is the man whom Thou shalt instruct, O Lord, and shalt teach him out of Thy Law

You asked me, Reverend Mother dear to me and devoted to God, to outline from the poor treasures of my heart some little thing that for the time being would be a help to devotion and would bring some light to your soul. Really, it is I who need such help, particularly as my life is not a shining example to others. Inwardly, I am not burning with tender devotion. Further, I have scarcely the knowledge necessary to do what you ask. Nevertheless, out of regard for your repeatedly expressed wishes, and anxious to oblige you, I have done what you so earnestly prayed of me.

Let me, however, beg of Your Beatitude, dear most holy Mother not to think so much of what I have written, as of my good and kind intentions. Please look for the truths of which I speak rather than for beauty of expression. Where I do not come up to your expectations, pardon me, and put my shortcomings down, please, to lack of time and stress of business.

:HAPTER I: TRUE SELF-KNOWLEDGE

he spouse of Christ who longs to become perfect must begin ʼith her own self. She must put aside and forget everything lse, entering into the secrecy of her own heart. When she has one this, let her sift thoroughly all her weaknesses, habits, ffections, actions and sins. She must weigh everything arefully, and make a complete examination of past and resent. Should she discover even the least imperfection, let her ʼeep in the bitterness of her heart.

legligence, passion, and malice are the three root causes of sin Cf. Bonaventure's Threefold Way.) When we realize, dear lother, that our sins and imperfections originate from one or ther of these three causes, we enter on the way to an exact nderstanding of ourselves; but unless in our recollection of ast offences we put our finger on the precise cause of each in, we shall never reach the goal of perfect self-knowledge.

'erfect self-knowledge, I feel sure, is the object you propose to ourself. You wish, helped by such knowledge, to bewail your ast transgressions. Since this is so you cannot do better than ɔ proceed as follows.

irst, discover by reflection whether you are occasionally or abitually negligent. Recollect whether the control of your heart ; slipshod and haphazard. Are you careless in the use of your me? Is the intention you propose to your self habitually nperfect? Examine yourself diligently on these three points, ecause it is of the utmost importance that you govern your ffections, that you spend your time profitably and that always nd in every action you have a good and becoming object or nd in view.

Recollect how negligent you have been in the discharge of your uties: prayer, reading, and the like. Remember that the performance of these tasks and the cultivation of these practices demand your best energies if you are to produce and bring forth worthy fruit in due season. (Cf. Ps. i, 3.) It is of little avail to excel in one practice if you fail in the others.

Go on with the examination, recalling to mind your neglect of penitential exercises, your negligent attitude towards temptation and sin, as well as your general disregard for the means of perfection. To reach the Promised Land you must weep with grief at the thought of the sins you have committed. Further, you must resist temptations to evil, and you must "advance from virtue to virtue." (Ps. lxxxiii, 8.) Take to heart these principles, and you will be able to form a true estimate of your negligence.

Should you wish to pursue the subject and know yourself still better, take another look at yourself and ask whether your interior promptings tend towards pleasure, curiosity or vanity.

There is an evident weakness for pleasures of sense when a religious looks eagerly for what is sweet, for instance, delicious dishes. A similar weakness prevails when she is anxious for what is soft and comforting: fine clothing, for example, or things gratifying to or soothing to the flesh, as, for example, luxuries. You may know for a certainty that the handmaid of the Lord is a victim of inquisitiveness when she longs to fathom secrets, to gaze on pleasurable and beautiful objects, and to possess unusual and precious things. To seek the esteem and the good opinion of others, to look for the praise of men and to be anxious for the honors in their gifts: the presence of any or all of these tendencies in a spouse of Christ shows a vain mind. O handmaid of Christ, shun these proclivities as poison, for they are the springs or founts of evil!

You will complete the examination and understand yourself thoroughly if you discover whether you nourish or have nourished within your breast the malice of anger, envy, or sloth. Please pay attention to what I have to say.

Anger or irascibility is surely nourished in the heart when the thoughts, whisperings, spoken words, emotions, gestures or features of a religious are tinged with even the slightest coloring of animosity or indignation against another. Envy holds sway in a man when he feels joyful at another's misfortune or is sad when better things come his neighbor's way. The envious man rejoices at another s troubles and is cast down when all goes well with him. Sloth cannot be mistaken. It is sloth that inclines the religious to lukewarmness, drowsiness, unpunctuality, laziness, negligence, remissness, dissoluteness, lack of devotion, sadness, or weariness. The spouse of God must have a holy horror of these things and avoid them as deadly poison. In them lurks the ruin of both soul and body.

O handmaid, beloved of God, if perfect self-knowledge is your aim, reflect! "Enter into your heart and learn to value yourself at your proper worth. Discuss with yourself what you are, what you were, what you ought to be, and what you can be. Note what you were originally, what you are now through your own fault, what on the contrary good efforts ought to have made you, and what you still may be by correspondence with grace." (St. Bernard, The Inter. Dwelling xxxvi)

Listen, dear Mother, to the Prophet David proposing himself as an example to you. "I meditated in the night with my own heart and I was exercised and I swept my spirit" (Ps. lxxvi, 7.) He meditated with his heart; do the same yourself. He swept his spirit; sweep yours. Cultivate this field. Fix your eyes upon your own self.

Without doubt, if you keep up this exercise you will find the hidden treasure of priceless worth. (Cf. St. Matt, xiii, 44) A golden increase will come to you. More and more will your knowledge be widened and your wisdom strengthened. Be faithful to this exercise and the eye of your heart will be cleansed, the acumen of your mind developed, and your intelligence enlarged. If you do not know your own dignity and condition, you cannot value anything at its proper worth. One must first take thought upon one's own soul if the angelic and divine natures are to be correctly estimated and esteemed. If you are not able to reflect upon yourself, how will you be fitted t investigate the things above you? "If you are not yet worthy to enter the first tabernacle, how will you have the effrontery to enter the Holy of Holies?" (Richard of St. Victor)

If you wish to be lifted up to the second and third heavens (Cf. I Cor. xii, 2), you must pass through the first; that is, you must pass through your own heart. How this is possible, and how it ought to be done, I have already explained. In addition, here is piece of excellent and illuminating advice from St. Bernard: "If you are earnestly desirous of uprightness and perfection, examine continually and think well on your way of living. Notice how much you advance in virtue and how much you fall away. Examine your conduct and the sentiments that inspire you. Loo and see how like to God you are, and how unlike! How near to God, and alas, how far away from Him!" (S. Bernard, Meditations, Ch. v, 14)

Oh, how dangerous a thing it is for a religious to wish to know much and yet not to know himself! How near death and perdition is that religious who is keenly interested in getting to the bottom of things, or who as a spiritual guide lives to solve the doubts and perplexities of distressed souls, yet does not know himself nor his own state! (Cf. S. Bonav, Soliloquium, i, 2. O my God, whence comes such blindness in a religious?

I will tell you. I have the reason at my finger-tips. A man whose mind is distraught in its anxieties for others has no memory for himself. His imagination is so clouded with pictures of other persons and things that he cannot form an idea of his own state. The allurements of unlawful passions so fascinate him that he never gets back to himself with a longing for interior sweetness and spiritual joy. Things of sense so possess his whole being that he can no longer enter into himself as the image of God. Thus entirely wretched, not knowing himself, he knows nothing (Cf. S. Aug., de Ordine I, 3.)

Put everything else aside and learn well and bear in mind what you are. For such self-knowledge St. Bernard prayed: “God, grant that I may know nothing if I do not know my own self.” (S. Bernard, Serm. de Diversis, I)

CHAPTER II: TRUE HUMILITY

To see personal defects aright a man must feel himself "humbled under the mighty hand of God." (I Pet. v, 6.) I admonish you, therefore, O handmaid of Christ, the moment you realise your failings, to humble yourself in abject humility and acknowledge to yourself your utter worthlessness. "Humility," says St. Bernard, "is a virtue which prompts a man possessing an exact knowledge of himself to estimate himself and his powers as dross" (S. Bern., Degrees of Humility, i,2.)

Our holy Father St. Francis possessed this virtue. He considered himself the meanest of men, and from his entrance into religion even unto the end, he loved and cherished humility. Humility compelled St. Francis to leave the world. Humility drove him in beggar's garb through the streets of Assisi. Because he was humble, he served the lepers. For the same reason, when preaching he made public his sins. His humility caused him to ask others to upbraid him for his faults (S. Bonav , Life of St. Francis, Ch. ii.)

You ought to learn this virtue, dear Mother, from the example of the Son of God. "Learn from me," Jesus says, "because I am meek and humble of heart." (Matt, xi, 29.) To excel in virtue and yet not to practise humility is simply to "carry dust before the wind," says St. Gregory (S. Greg., I Homil. on the Gospel, vii, 4.) As "pride is the beginning of all sin," (Eccl. x, 15) so humility is the foundation of all virtue. Learn to be really humble and not, as the hypocrite, humble merely in appearance.

Speaking of hypocrites Ecclesiasticus says, "There is one that humbleth himself wickedly and his interior is full of deceit" (Eccl. xix, 23.) "The truly humble man," says St. Bernard, "does not desire to be advertised as a humble man, but wishes to be reputed and considered worthless" (S. Bernard, Sermons on the Canticle, xvi, 10.)

o, Reverend Mother, if you wish to be perfectly humble, you ıust advance by three stages.

he first stage is thought upon God as the Author of all good. Ve must say to ourselves, "O Lord, Thou hast wrought all our orks in us"(Is. xxvi, 12.) Because this is really so, you must ttribute every good work to Him and not to yourself. Bear in ıind that "you in your own might and in the strength of your own and" (Cf. Deut. viii, 17) have not attained to all the good things ou possess. "It is the Lord who made us and not we ourselves" Cf. Ps. xcix, 3.)

uch thoughts completely upset the pride of those who say, Our mighty hand and not the Lord hath done all these things" Deut. xxxii, 27.) It was pride such as this which caused Lucifer) be expelled from the glory of heaven. Lucifer would not ealise that he was made from nothing, but taking delight in his omeliness and beauty, and remarking how "every precious tone was his covering," (Cf. Ezek. xxviii, 13) he exalted himself ı his pride. And because "pride goes before a fall," (Cf. Prov. xix, 23) in the twinkling of an eye he was hurled headlong from is pride of place down to the lowest depths of abject misery. hus the most exalted of angels became the most depraved of emons.

h, how many children of Lucifer there are today, men and omen, imitators of Lucifer! Sons and daughters of pride whom od in His patience endures! "Pride," says St. Bernard, "is less ateful in the rich than in the poor" (S. Bernard, Sermon liv, 8.) he handmaid of Christ, therefore, must always practise umility, since she is to fill the place vacated by a rejected ngel. It matters little whether the creature is an angel or a man; umility alone renders both the one and the other pleasing to od.

If you are not humble, do not imagine for a moment that your virginity is pleasing to God. Mary would not have been made the Mother of God if she had been a proud woman. "I make bold to say," writes St. Bernard, "that without humility not even Mary's virginity would have pleased God" (S. Bernard, Hom. I in S. Luke, i, 26.) Humility is a great virtue. Without it not only is there no virtue, but that which might have been virtue is vitiated and turns to pride.

The second stage is the remembrance of Christ. You must remember that Christ was humiliated even to a most ignominious death (Cf. Phil, ii, 8.) So humiliated was He that He was reputed a leper. Hence Isaiah said, "We have thought Him as it were, a leper, and as one struck by God" (Is. liii, 4.) Christ was humiliated to such an extent that in His day nothing was considered viler than He. "In humiliation," continues the prophet "His judgment was taken away" (Is. liii, 8.) The burden of the prophet's thought is this: So great was His humility, and so lowly did He make Himself that no one could form a correct judgment of Him, no one could believe that He was God.

If then "Our Lord and Master" Himself said: "The servant is not greater than his Lord, the disciple is not above his master" (John xiii, 16; Matt, x, 24), so you, if you are the handmaid of Christ and His disciple, must be lowly, prepared to be despised and humbled. What is more contemptible in God's eyes than the religious who with a humble garment covers a proud heart? Of what use is that Christian who sees His Lord humbled and despised, yet himself "exalts his heart and walks in great matters and in wonderful things above himself" (Cf. Ps. cxxx, i)?

The Most High God became as the least of all, and the immense Creator became a little creature; yet a filthy worm, a mere handmaid of Christ, "exalts and magnifies herself" (Cf. Ps. ix, 18.) What could be more detestable! What could be more deserving of punishment! Of such the blessed St. Augustine xclaims in this way: "O ye bags of carrion, why do you swell ourselves up so? O ye putrid festers, why are you puffed up? low dare the members of a body be proud when the Head is umble?" (S. Aug., Serm. 304.) A forceful way of emphasizing ne unseemliness of such behaviour!

he third stage by which you must advance, if you would ecome really humble, is by close acquaintanceship with your wn self. You become acquainted with yourself when you ealise "whence you have come and whither you are going" (S. ern., Meditations i, I.) Consider then whence you come, and ake it to heart that you are the slime of the earth. You have vallowed in sin and are an exile from the happy kingdom of leaven. Thoughts such as these will quell the spirit of pride and rive it away somewhat. Thoughts like these will persuade you o cry out with the three youths mentioned in the book of Daniel, We are brought low in all the earth, this day for our sins" (Dan. i, 37.)

ake now the other point. Where are you going? You are slowly noving towards corruption and elemental ashes. "Dust thou art nd unto dust shalt thou return" (Gen. iii, 19.) "Why be proud, ou who are but dust and ashes?" (Cf. Ecclesiasticus x, 9.) oday here, tomorrow gone! In good health today, a mass of ilments tomorrow! Wise today, possibly an idiot tomorrow! ich—and rich in virtue as you read these lines—tomorrow it nay easily be said that you could find yourself a miserable, vretched beggar! Show me the Christian who will dare to extol imself when he realizes that he is hemmed in on all sides by so nany miseries and possible misfortunes!

earn, consecrated virgins, to have a humble mind and to walk vith a humble mien. Be humble in your tastes and ways and ress. It is humility, remember, that softens God's anger and enders us fit subjects for His holy grace. The greater thou art," emarks Ecclesiasticus, "the more humble thyself in all things, and thou shalt find grace before God" (Ecclesiasticus iii, 20.) This is how Mary found favour with God. Her own words are: "He hath regarded the humility of His handmaid" (Luke i, 48.)

There is no reason for surprise in this. Humility prepares the way for God's grace and frees the mind from all vanity. It is for this reason that St. Augustine says, "The less the pride, the more the love" (S. Aug., De Civit. Dei, VIII. 12.) Just as the waters crowd into the valleys, so the graces of the Holy Spirit fill the humble. And to continue the comparison, just as the greater the incline the quicker the water flows, so the more the heart bends under humility, the nearer we are to God. Thus it is easy for the man who is humble of heart to approach near to God and to beg His Grace. "The prayer of him that humbleth himself," Ecclesiasticus tells us, "shall pierce the clouds: and till it come nigh *[to the Most High]* he will not be comforted" (Ecclesiasticus xxxv, 21.) For "the Lord will do the will of them that fear Him, and He will hear their prayers" (Ps. cxliv, 19.)

Dear children of God and handmaids of Christ, be always humble. "Never allow pride to dominate your hearts" (Cf. Tob. iv, 14.) You have in Jesus Christ Our Lord a humble Master. Your mistress, Our Blessed Lady and Queen of us all, was humble. Be humble because St. Francis your Father was humble. Be humble because your Mother, St. Clare, was a model of humility.

Be humble almost to excess, and let patience be the test of your humility, for humility is perfected by patience. Indeed there is no humility without patience. Listen to the words of St. Augustine: "It is easy to place a veil over the head and to cover the eyes, to wear poor and wretched clothes, and to walk with the head cast down, but it is patience that proves a man to be really humble" (S. Aug., Epist., 17.) "In thy humiliation," says Ecclesiasticus, "keep patience" (Ecclesiasticus ii, 4.)

Alas—and I speak with sorrow—there are many of us who would lead proud lives in the cloister, yet we were lowly enough in the world. St. Bernard realised this and voiced his complaint: "It grieves me very much to see many who trod beneath their feet the pomps of the world come into the school of humility the better to learn the ways of pride. Under the aegis of a mild and humble master they wax arrogant, and they become more impatient in the cloister than they were in the world. What is still worse, very many will not suffer themselves to be held of little worth in the house of God, although in their own circle they could not have been anything but lowly, nay, even contemptible" (S. Bern. Homil. iv, 10.)

I recommend you, therefore, dear Mother, to be solicitous for your daughters. Teach your daughters who have consecrated themselves to God to guard their virginity by humility, and to keep themselves humble by the practice of their virginity. "Virginity associated with humility is like a precious stone in a gold setting," says St. Bernard. "What is there so beautiful as the union of virginity with humility? How indescribably pleasing to God is the soul in which humility enhances virginity and virginity embellishes humility." (S. Bern. Homil. Missus est, i, 5.)

Lastly, dear Mother, please take the following advice from me, your brother. It will please you. Avoid a proud sister as you would avoid a viper; keep clear of the arrogant nun as though she were a devil. Look upon the companionship of the proud as some thing that is a virulent poison. Why? I will tell you why. A rather clever writer has left us the following pen picture of a proud man. "The proud man is unbearable. He is too loud in dress, pompous in his bearing, stiff-necked, unnaturally harsh of countenance, stern-eyed, ever on the lookout for the first places, wishful to outstrip his betters, boastful in everything, and devoid of all ideas of respect and proper reverence" (Prosper, Contemp. Life, viii, I.)

“He that hath fellowship with the proud,” says Ecclesiasticus, “shall put on pride.” (Cf Ecclesiasticus xiii, I.) O dear child of God, spouse of Christ, and virgin consecrated to the Lord, if you would avoid the risk of falling into the ways of the proud, shun the companionship of the proud.

HAPTER III: PERFECT POVERTY

overty is another of the virtues necessary if we would be holy nto perfection. Our Lord bears witness to this in the Gospel of t. Matthew: "If thou wilt be perfect, go sell what thou hast and ive to the poor" (Matt, xix, 21.) Since the fullness of Gospel erfection is found in poverty, no one should imagine that he as scaled the summits of perfection if he has not become an dept in the practice of evangelical poverty. Hugh of St. Victor ells us that "no matter how many practices of perfection are ound among religious, unless there is a love for poverty their fe cannot be considered fully perfect" (Cf. Expos. Reg. S. Aug., Sq.)

wo motives may be suggested that are capable of impelling ot merely a religious, but even an ordinary man to a love of overty. The first is the irreproachable example of Our Divine ord. The second is the priceless divine promise.

et us take the first motive. The love and the example of Our ivine Lord, Jesus Christ, ought to excite in you, His handmaid, love of poverty. Christ was born poor, lived poor, and died oor. Realise and bear in mind that Christ gave you this vonderful example of poverty in order to induce you to become friend of poverty. Our Lord Jesus Christ was so poor at birth nat He had neither shelter, nor clothing, nor food. In lieu of a ouse He had to be content with a stable. A few wretched rags id duty for His clothes. For food He had milk from the Virgin's reast.

was meditation on this poverty of Christ that roused the heart f St. Paul and caused him to exclaim, "You know the grace of ur Lord Jesus Christ, that being rich He became poor for our akes, that through His poverty we might be rich" (Cf. II Cor. viii, .) St. Bernard speaking of this same poverty says, "An eternal nd copious abundance of riches existed in Heaven. Poverty, however, was not to be found there, though it abounded and was superabundant on earth. Alas! man did not know its worth. The Son of God, though, loved poverty, and desired it, and came down from Heaven and took it as his own possession in order to make it precious in our eyes" (S. Bern. Serm. for Christmas Eve I, 5.)

All His life long, Jesus Christ Our Lord was an example of poverty. Let me tell you, O holy virgin, and all you who profess poverty, let me tell you how poor the Son of God and King of Angels was while He lived in this world. He was so poor that oftentimes He did not know which way to turn for lodging. Frequently, He and His Apostles were compelled to wander out of the city and sleep where they could. It is with reference to such a happening that St. Mark the Evangelist writes, "Having viewed all things round about, when now the eventide was come, He went out to Bethany with the twelve" (Mark xi, 11.)

These words St. Bede explains as follows: "After looking all around and making enquiries as to whether any one was prepared to give Him hospitality—for He was so poor that no one looked upon Him with pleasure—He could not find a dwelling open to Him in the town" (Cf. S. Bede, Vol. V. p. 125.) In a similar strain St. Matthew writes: "The foxes have holes and the birds of the air nests; but the Son of Man hath nowhere to lay His head" (Matt, viii, 20; Cf. Expos. S. Bonav.)

Added to the poverty of His birth and life was the poverty of the death of the King of Angels. "All you" who have taken the vow of poverty, "stop and consider for a moment" (Lamentations, i, 12) how poor the Lord of all was made for your sakes. Look at His poverty as He dies. His executioners stripped and robbed Him of everything He possessed. He was robbed of His clothes, I repeat it, when the executioners "divided His garments between them, and for His vesture cast lots." (Cf. Matt, xxvii, 35; Cf. Ps. xxi, 19.) He was robbed of body and soul when, as He uccumbed to His most bitter sufferings, His soul was separated om His body in the pangs of death. His persecutors deprived nd robbed Him of His divine glory when they refused "to glorify im as God," (Cf. Rom. i, 21) and instead treated Him as a ommon criminal.

They have stripped me of my glory," (Cf. Job xix, 9) complains oly Job in a moment of prophecy. Drawing a lesson from the ompelling example of Christ's poverty, St. Bernard writes: Think of the poor man Christ! There is no house for Him at His irth, so they lay Him in a manger, between an ox and an ass. ook at Him wrapped in wretched swaddling clothes! Think of im a fugitive on the rough road to Egypt! Think of Him riding on n ass! Think of His poverty as He hangs on the cross" (S. ern. Serm. Easter III, I.)

fter realizing that the God of Gods, the Lord of the World, the ing of Heaven, the only begotten Son of God has borne the urden of such dire poverty, where is the Christian, where is the bstinate and benighted religious who still loves riches and espises poverty? "It is a great, a heinous crime that a vile and ontemptible worm, for whom the God of Majesty and Lord of All ecame poor, should desire to be rich." So says St. Bernard, nd he adds: "Let the godless pagan covet riches. Let the Jew ho has received the promise of the land look for the fulfilment f the promise and for the possession of the land" (S. Bern. erm. All Saints I. 7.)

ut the maiden consecrated to God, the maiden who lives mong Christ's poor and whose profession is poverty, how can he look for the riches of earth? How, pray, can a daughter of ne poor man of Assisi, a maiden who has promised to imitate ne poverty of her holy Mother St. Clare, search for earthly iches?

Beyond all measure of belief, dear Mother, are we in our avarice put to shame. Although professing poverty, we have bartered away poverty for avarice. Although the Son of God "became poor for our sakes," (1 Cor. viii, 9) we are solicitous for what is not allowed us. We try to obtain what the Rule strictly forbids.

In commending perfect Gospel poverty to you, let me insist on the following well-known fact: The more you are attached to the poverty you profess, and the more you practise evangelical poverty, the more will you abound in spiritual and temporal treasures. If you go the contrary way, if you set no value on the poverty you have made your own by profession, then of a certainty will you experience most constant spiritual and temporal need.

That one-time poor woman, Mary the Mother of the poverty-stricken Jesus, sang: "He hath filled the hungry with good things and the rich he hath sent empty away" (Luke i, 53.) The most holy Psalmist expressed the same thought: "The rich have wanted, and have suffered hunger, but they that seek the Lord shall not be deprived of any good" (Ps. xxx, ii.) Did you never read, did you never hear what Christ the Lord said of poverty to His Apostles? It occurs in the Gospel of St. Matthew. "Be not solicitous, therefore, saying, what shall we eat, or, what shall we drink. Your Father knoweth that you have need of all these things" (Matt, vi, 31–32.) Here is something else He said. It is from St. Luke. "When I sent you without purse, and scrip, and shoes, did you lack anything? But they said: Nothing" (Luke xxii 35–36.)

Living among hard-hearted unbelieving persons, Christ did not find it difficult to attend to His disciples' wants. Is it any wonder then that He is able to supply the wants of the Friars Minor, and the Poor Ladies, who, living among a faithful and Christian people, profess and imitate a poverty akin to that of the postles? "Cast, therefore, all your care upon Him, for He areth for you" (1 Pet. v, 7.)

ince the fatherly care and solicitude of God for us is so itense, should not our anxious longing for temporal things ause us to marvel? Should it not astound us that we are eaten p with desire for vain and empty things? Why, when God ccupies Himself with our welfare, do we trouble ourselves so bout things of wealth and things of little concern? I can find no ther explanation than that we have become avaricious. varice—avarice, the mother of confusion and damnation—has ken hold of us.

/e may give no other reason than that we have turned away ur affections from God, our Salvation (Cf. Deut. xxxii, 15.) The re of Divine Love has become extinguished in us. We have ooled. Love for God has frozen within us. If we were really ervent and had really stripped ourselves of earthly things, we hould follow the poverty-stricken Christ (S. Jer. Ep. cxxv, 20.) /hen men become excessively hot, they are accustomed to trip themselves of their clothes. The proof of our lack of love nd of our great coolness is the attraction which worldly goods ossess for us.

) my God, how can we be so harsh with Christ? "He went forth om His own country," from Heaven, "from His own kinsfolk," ie Angels, "from the house of His Father," (Cf. Gen. xii, i) from lis Father's bosom, and for us became poor, abject and espised! Yet we are unwilling to give up a wretched and oisome world for Him. We leave the world in body, it is true, ut in heart and mind and inclination we give ourselves up to nd are wholly absorbed by the world.

) blessed servant of God, recall the poverty of Our Lord Jesus :hrist, poor for our sake! Impress on your heart the poverty of our Father, the poor little man Francis. Meditate on the poverty of your holy Mother St. Clare. Cleave to poverty and practise it zealously and courageously. Embrace the Lady Poverty and pray God that for Our Lord's sake you may never wish to love anything else under heaven save poverty. Keep your heart free from love of honours, temporal things, and riches. Strive diligently to live up to the holy poverty you have vowed.

It is a waste of energy to possess and to love riches. To have one's heart set on riches and yet to be poor is a dangerous business. To be rich and yet not to love one's riches is too wearisome. The advantage, the security, the delight of life and the act of perfect virtue is neither to possess riches nor to have any fondness for riches. Therefore, Our Lord's example and counsel ought to prompt and inspire every Christian to love poverty.

O blessed poverty, which makes those who love it beloved of God and secure even in this world! "For him who has nothing in the world on which his heart is set, there exists nothing of the world to fear" (S. Greg. Moral. Book X, xxi, 39.) So says St. Gregory. In the lives of the Fathers we read that there was a certain poor monk who owned a mat. At night he put half of it under him and the other half he used as a coverlet. Once when it was very cold, the superior of the monastery heard the poor monk praying: "I give thanks, O my God," he prayed, "because there are very many rich men in prison, many in irons, many in the stocks. But I, like an emperor and lord, may stretch my legs and go whither I wish" (Life of John the Almsg., xx.)

There now; I have done with the first point, the example of poverty. The second motive to inspire a love of poverty is the promise, the priceless promise of Christ. O good Jesus, "rich unto all," (Rom. x, 19) who can worthily realize, tell, or write of that marvellous heavenly glory which Thou hast promised to give to Thy poor? The practice of voluntary poverty earns the reward of the beatific vision (Cf. S. Greg. Hom., II Book, xxxvii,

, and the right to enter into the palace of the Power of God (Cf. 's. lxx, 16.) Votaries of voluntary poverty merit a place in the ternal dwellings. They have a right to enter God's brilliantly luminated mansions, and they become citizens of the city built nd fashioned by God.

'hou, O my God, with Thy own Blessed Mouth hast promised iem this eternal reward! "Blessed are the poor in spirit, for ieirs is the Kingdom of Heaven" (Matt, v, 6.) The Kingdom of leaven, O my Lord Jesus Christ, is nothing else than Thou, 'hyself, Who art "the King of Kings and Lord of Lords" (I Tim. vi, 5.) As reward, as the price of their labour, as a complete and erfect joy, Thou wilt give to Thy voluntary poor even the ossession of Thyself.

'hey will rejoice in possessing Thee. They will find delight in 'hee. They will, at last, find complete satisfaction in Thee. For he poor shall eat and shall be filled; and they shall praise the ord that seek Him; their hearts shall live for ever and ever" (Ps. xi, 27.) Amen.

CHAPTER IV: SILENCE

"In the multitude of words there shall not want sin" (Prov. x, 19.) I quote from the Book of Proverbs.

Obviously, a religious aiming to perfect his ways will find silence a very helpful virtue. To speak seldom, and then but briefly, prevents sin. Where there is too much talk, God is in one way or another offended, and reputations suffer. On the other hand, let only the virtue of silence come into its own, and people get their due. If we deal fairly with one another and practise the virtue of justice, we establish the bond of peace. This means that where silence is observed, the fruits of peace are gathered as easily as fruit is gathered from a heavily-laden tree.

Of all places in the world peace is essential in the cloister. Silence is of paramount importance in the life of a religious, because by means of silence peace of mind and body is preserved. Expounding on the virtue of silence, Isaiah the prophet said: "The work of justice shall be peace, and the service of justice shall be quietness" or silence (Is. xxxii, 17; Cf. S. Greg. Moral. VII, xvii, 58; S. Bern. Epis. lxxxix, 2.) It is as though he said: The nature of silence is such that it acts as a preservative of the godly virtue Justice. It encourages peaceful ways and enables men to live in peace and harmony.

We may lay it down as a principle that unless a man diligently "sets a guard to his tongue," (Cf. Ps. xxxviii, 24. Ps. cxl, 3) he must lose all the graces he has acquired and necessarily and quickly fall into evil ways. "The tongue," wrote the Apostle St. James, "is indeed a little member and boasteth great things." It is "a fire, a world of iniquity" (James iii, 5, 6.) According to the commentators, St. James' meaning is that almost all evil deeds are inspired or perpetrated by the tongue.

shall now briefly enumerate for you, dear sister, the sins into
hich we are liable to fall if we do not keep a strict guard over
ie tongue. A loose and glib tongue easily becomes the vehicle
f blasphemy and murmuring. The tongue that wags will be
uilty of perjury, lying and detraction. The sin of flattery is easy
› it. Easy as well are cursing, abusive language, quarrelsome
alk, and words which mockingly slander virtue and entice to evil
eeds. Scandalous gossip, vain boasting, the divulging of
ecrets, idle threats, rash promises, frequent and silly chattering
nd scurrilous conversation: all these sins come lightly,
moothly, and easily from an unguarded tongue.

o be unable to hold her tongue ought to make an ordinary
voman blush. When the woman is a woman consecrated to
iod, a woman who knows the magnitude of the evils following
n too easy a use of the tongue, then that woman's life is
narred by a gross blemish. I have no hesitation in saying that it
s useless for a religious to take pride in the virtue which
haracterizes her, if by too much talking she observes the rule
f silence only in the breach. "If any man think himself to be
eligious, not bridling his tongue but deceiving his own heart,
nis man's religion is vain" (James i, 26.)

) amiable spouses of Jesus Christ, let us look up to Mary, Our
.ady and Mother, since all virtues are reflected in Mary. Helped
y the Holy Gospels, let us look upon her and learn how to keep
ilence. St. Luke records that Mary spoke seldom and with but
ew people. From him we learn that twice she spoke with the
ngel (Luke i, 34 & 38), twice with her Divine Son (Luke ii, 48;
ohn ii, 3), twice with her cousin St. Elisabeth (Luke i, 40 & 46
q), and once to the waiters at the Marriage Feast (John ii, 5.)
hought on Our Lady's spare use of words will do us good. It
vill cause us to blush. We are too talkative. With us it is talk,
alk, talk, yet all the time silence is the great and useful thing.

Silence begets compunction of heart, and here is its first usefu purpose. When a man is silent he falls to thinking and brooding over his manner of life (Cf. Ps. cxviii, 59.) This enables him quickly to see his many defects and the little progress he has made in the spiritual life, and soon compunction holds him captive. David tells us this: "I was mute and humbled, and kept silence from good things, and my sorrow was renewed" (Ps. xxxviii, 3.)

Silence has another advantage: It shows that man belongs to a better world. If a man lives in Germany and yet does not speak German, we naturally conclude that he is not a German. So too we rightly conclude that a man who does not give himself up to worldly conversation is not of this world, although he lives therein. The argument is conclusive. St. John the Evangelist, quoting St. John the Baptist, has told us: "He that is of the earth of the earth he is, and of the earth he speaketh" (John iii, 31. C S. Bern. Epis. lxxviii, 4.)

The religious who wants to cultivate the habit of silence cannot do better than to shun the company of his fellows and lead the life of a solitary. When he has lifted himself out of himself, God should be his only companion and comforter. A solitary and quiet life should be his aim. To have God as his companion should suffice, and he should look for neither comfort from nor companionship with men. "He shall sit solitary," avoiding the companionship of his fellows, "and shall hold his peace," (Lamentations, iii, 28) and meditating on heavenly things, he should lift himself above himself and revel in the sweetness of heavenly delights.

To be perfectly virtuous, a religious must practise silence. Silence is essential to the spouses of Jesus Christ and to women consecrated to God. Religious women should be particularly sparing with their words. Their words should be "precious" (Cf. I Kings iii, I.) Talking should cause them to blush, and they should never speak except in extreme necessity. St. Jerome may be quoted very aptly here: "Let the words of a virgin be few and seemly, and precious rather by their reticence than by their eloquence" (S. Jer., Epis. i, 19.)

One of the great philosophers of old taught in the same way: "To be perfect, I would counsel you to speak but little and only on rare occasions. When a rare occasion occurs, remember too, to speak scarcely above a whisper" (Seneca, Ep. xl.) O you talkative girls, you chatterboxes, you garrulous nuns! I have a story for you which, if you take it to heart, will teach you what you must do if you would learn to keep silence.

In the lives of the Fathers (Migne Patr. V, Book iv, 7), it is related that a certain abbot, Agathon by name, kept a stone in his mouth to prevent his talking. For three years he continued the practice until at last he learned how to hold his tongue. Take this lesson to heart: tie a stone to your tongue. Fasten your tongue to your palate. "Put thy fingers on thy mouth" (Judges xviii, 19) and learn to keep silent. Remember always that it ill becomes a woman vowed to Christ to look for conversation with any one except her Spouse Jesus Christ.

Talk, therefore, only on rare occasions, and let your conversations be short. Use but few words. Speak in fear and trembling and in all modesty. Above all "scarcely ever speak in your own cause," (Cf. Ecclesiasticus xxxii, 10), that is, in your own defence. Cover your face with a veil of bashful modesty. Sew your lips together with the threads of rule and discipline. Let your words be few, for "in the multiplicity of words there shall not want sin" (Prov. x, 19.) Let your conversation be useful, modest and humble. Never speak an idle word, because "every idle word that men shall speak, they shall render an account for it in the day of judgment" (Matt, xii, 36.) Speaking of idle words, it may be noticed with St. Gregory that "an idle word is one that the speaker uses without necessity or with no advantage to the hearer" (S. Greg., Moral., VII, xvii, 58.)

It is always better and more useful to be silent than to speak. As witness of which truth let me quote a saying of Xenocrates, one of the philosophers of old: "I have often repented because I spoke, but never have I been sorry that I held my peace." (Val. Max. vii Dict. Fact. Memorab., 2.)

HAPTER V: THE PRACTICE OF PRAYER

he religious whose heart is cold and tepid leads a wretched nd useless life; nay, the tepid religious, the religious who does ot pray fervently and assiduously, scarcely lives at all. His body es, but in the sight of God it harbors a dead soul. It follows ien that prayerful habits are essential if the spouse of Christ is achieve her desires and advance towards perfection. The ractice of prayer is a virtue of such efficacy that of itself it can ompletely subdue all the cunning devices of its implacable nemy, the devil. It is the devil and the devil alone who prevents e servant of God from soaring above herself even unto the eavens. There is, then, no reason for surprise that the religious ho is not devoted to the practice of constant prayer succumbs equently to temptation.

t. Isidore realised this truth, for he says: "Prayer is the remedy hen temptations to sin rage in the heart. Whenever you are mpted to sin, pray, and pray earnestly. Frequent prayer nders powerless the assaults of vice" (S. Isid. III Sent, viii, I.) ur Lord gives similar advice in the Gospel: "Watch and pray at ye enter not into temptation" (Matt xxvi, 41.)

evout prayer is so powerful that it enables a man to win hatever he wants. Winter and summer, when times are tormy, when times are fair, night and day, Sunday and londay, in days of health, in the hour of illness, in youth and old ge, standing, sitting and walking, in choir and out of choir: in a ord, never need the efficacy of prayer fail. Indeed, at times, iore than the very world itself its worth may be gained by one our of prayer. By one little devout prayer it is possible for a ian to gain Heaven.

shall now discuss the nature of prayer. Probably, in this matter am more in need of information than you are! Still, insofar as the Lord inspires me, I shall tell you in what way and manner you should pray.

I would have you know, O worthy handmaid of God, that three conditions are requisite for perfect prayer. When you settle down to pray, close your senses to every sensation, and with your body and soul absolutely intent on what you are doing, ponder in silence with a sorrowful and contrite heart on all your past, present, and possible wretched efforts. Reflect seriously, in the first place, on the many grave sins you have committed from day to day. Call to mind how you have neglected so many opportunities for doing good—opportunities that came your way since your entrance into religion, and opportunities that were given you before you took the veil. Think of the many and wonderful graces you have lost (Cf. St. Bonaventure, The Threefold Way, II, 2.) Once you were near to God; realise how today sin keeps you far from Him. Bring home to yourself the fact that you have become unlike to God, yet there was a day when you were conformed to His very image and likeness. Your soul was once beautiful; today it is ugly and foul. Think on these facts.

Now turn your thoughts on what the future has in store for you. Whither will sin eventually "lead you"? "To the very gates of hell!" Remember that there is "a day of "dreadful "judgment." What is likely to befall you? Do not forget "the eternal fires of hell" (S. Bern. Medit.) How will your sins be punished?

Your reflection should move you to strike your breast with the humble publican (Cf. Luke xviii, 13.) "Groaning in heart, you should cry out your sorrow" (Cf. Ps xxxvii, 9) with the Prophet David, and in company with Mary Magdalene you should "wash the feet" of the Lord "with your tears" (Cf. Luke vii, 38.) There should be no end to your tears, for beyond all bounds have you offended your sweet Jesus by your sins.

;t. Isidore gives similar advice. "When we pray to God, we hould pray with groaning and weeping. This is possible if, when t prayer, we remember the sins we have committed, their xceptional gravity, and the awful torments we have deserved to uffer on account of our sins. Fear of those dread torments will nable us to pray with genuine sorrow" (S. Isidore, III Sent, vii, .)

ı this way we should begin our prayer. We should start our rayer with tears that spring from sincere regret and earnest ear.

'hanksgiving is the second requisite. Blessings received from ;od should call forth the humble thanks of the spouse of Christ. ;o too, should she thank God in all humility for the benefits yet ɔ accrue to her. In his epistle to the Colossians St. Paul lays tress on this part of prayer: "Be instant," he says, "in prayer, vatching in it with thanksgiving" (Col. iv, 2.) Nothing makes a nan so worthy of God's gifts as the constant offering of thanks ɔ God for gifts received.

Vriting to Aurelius, St. Augustine touches on this matter. "What etter thoughts," he asks, "can we have in our minds, what etter sentiments in our hearts than those of thanksgiving to ;od? What better words are given us to utter or to write than)eo Gratias? The idea of due thanksgiving could not be xpressed in fewer words. What other words could give greater leasure? No other two words are so full of meaning. What nore profitable than their use?" (S. Aug. Ep. xli.)

'ou must meditate, you must pray with a grateful heart. Thank ;od because He made you. Thank Him because He raised you o the Christian state. Thank God because He has forgiven you o many sins. Thank Him because, had He not taken care of ou, you would have fallen much lower (Cf. S. Bern. Serm. ii in ; Sund. after Pent.) Thanksgiving is due from you because God has taken you out of the world; thanks to Him you will die in religion. You should thank God because He has chosen you to live the life of a religious in the highest and most perfect religious state. You have no worry, nor any anxiety. He keeps you from harm, comforts you, and gives you all that you need.

Further motives for continual thanksgiving on your part arise from the fact that God took to Himself a human nature and became man for your sake. It was for you that He was circumcised and baptized. For you He lived His poor life. For you He went poorly clothed, was humbled and despised. All His fastings, hungers, thirst, labours, and fatigues He endured for your sake. For you He wept. Love for you prompted Him to give you His Most Holy Body to eat and His Most Precious Blood to drink. In anguish for you He bled from His very pores in the Garden. For you He was struck in the face, spat upon, mocked and scourged. For love of you He was fastened to the cross. He was wounded for your sake. He was done to death by the most cruel and agonizing crucifixion because of His love for you.

It was because He so loved you that He paid such a price for your redemption. He was buried, He rose from the dead, He ascended into Heaven, and He sent the Holy Spirit into the world simply because of His promise to give you and His chosen ones the Kingdom of Heaven. Such motives should be sufficient inducement to you to make your prayer an act of thanksgiving. Remember too, that while acts of gratitude render prayer immeasurably efficacious, all prayer is valueless without the element of thanksgiving. “Ingratitude,” says St. Bernard, “is a parching wind which dries up the sources of piety, the dew of mercy, and the streams of grace” (S. Bern. Serm. li on the Canticle of Cant.)

This brings me to the third requisite of perfect prayer. You must in the act of prayer occupy yourself with and think of nothing else but what you are doing. It ill becomes a man to speak to

;od with his lips while in heart and mind he is far away from ;od. To pray half-heartedly—giving, say, half one's attention to hat one is doing and the remaining half to some business natter or other—is no prayer at all. Prayers made in such a way s this never reach the ear of God. In the 118th Psalm there ccurs the following line: "I cried with my whole heart: hear me,) Lord" (Ps. cxviii, 145.) St. Augustine discovers in this passage ie implication that "a heart divided obtains nothing" (S. Aug. on ame verse, Serm. xxix.)

Vhen at prayer, the servant of God should recollect herself and, aking her heart to herself, banish from it all solicitude for things f earth. Earthly desires should be put aside and all love of iends and family forgotten. All her thoughts and affections hould be turned inwards and she should give herself up wholly) the God to whom she prays.

'our spouse, Our Divine Lord, Jesus Christ, gave this counsel ı the Holy Gospel: "But thou, when thou shalt pray, enter into ıy chamber and, having shut the door, pray to thy Father in ecret" (Matt, vi, 6.) "To enter into your chamber" means to ecall and gather into the very inmost recesses of your heart all our thoughts, all your desires, and all your affections. You have shut the door" when you have your heart so well under control ıat no thought or wandering fantasy can thwart you in your levotions.

;t. Augustine's definition of prayer makes all this evident. Prayer," he says, "is the raising or turning of the mind to God by ıeans of loving and humble acts of affection" (S. Aug., The loly Spirit and the Soul, 50.)

.et me exhort you, most good Mother and handmaid of Jesus ;hrist, to "incline your ear to the words of my mouth." (Cf. Ps. liv, ii; Ps. lxxvii, I.) Do not be misled. Do not be deceived in any vay. Do not allow the sure and great fruits of prayer to slip from your grasp; do not throw away and so destroy the sweets of prayer. Let not the delights you may drink to the full in prayer be drunk to no purpose. Prayer is the well out of which sanctifying grace is drawn from the spring of the overflowing sweetness of the Most Blessed Trinity.

The Holy Prophet David, who knew all about this, said, "I opened my mouth, and panted" (Ps. cxviii, 131.) "David meant," says St. Augustine, "I opened my mouth in prayer, I begged by prayer. With reiterated prayers I knocked at the door of Heaven and thirsting for the grace of God I panted and drew in that heavenly grace" (S. Aug. on the same Psalm.)

I have already told you what prayer is, but I will tell it to you again. "Prayer is the raising or turning of the mind to God." Pay attention to what I am about to say if you wish to learn how to raise or turn your mind to God.

When you give yourself to prayer, you must recollect yourself and with your Beloved enter into your secret heart and there occupy yourself with Him alone. Forget everything else and with all your mind, heart, affections and desires, with all the devotion possible, lift yourself out of and above yourself (Cf. Lamentations, iii, 28.) Take care not to allow your mind to become remiss, but endeavour constantly, by the burning ardour of devotion, to mount upwards till you enter "into the place of the wonderful tabernacle, even to the house of God" (Ps. xli, 5.)

There, when with the eye of your soul you have caught sight of your Beloved, you should in one way and another "taste that the Lord is sweet" (Ps. xxxiii, 9), and learn how great is "the multitude of His sweetness" (Ps. xxx, 20.) You should rush to your Lover's embrace, and kiss Him with the lips of tenderest love. Then, indeed, will you be lifted out of yourself. You will be rapt even up to Heaven. You will be transformed wholly into hrist. At last, unable to restrain the raptures of your soul, you vill exclaim with David, "My soul refused to be comforted. I emembered God and I was delighted" (Ps. lxxvi, 3, 4.)

here are three ways in which the soul may be transported out f herself and elevated even unto God. In order then, dear nother, that you may learn how the heart may be lifted up igher and higher, and how prayer may inflame our love for God till more, I shall discuss these three methods.

surpassing intensity or excess of devotion is one. Deeply ooted, ever-increasing, admiring love is another. The third is xceeding great, exulting joy.

s for the first, it happens at times that owing to excess of evotion "the soul cannot contain herself. She is lifted up, rapt ut of herself and finally becomes transformed. When we are et alight by so great a fire of heavenly desire that everything of arth is changed into bitterness and becomes distasteful to us, nd at the same time the fires of the love of our inmost heart icrease in intensity beyond measure, the soul melts as though he were wax. She in some way becomes dissolved, and like ie fumes of fragrant incense she mounts high, until at length he gains her freedom away on the topmost summits of leaven" (Richard of St. Victor.) When this happens we are ompelled to exclaim with the Prophet David: "My flesh and my eart have fainted away. Thou art the God of my heart, and the God that is my portion forever" (Ps. lxxii, 26.)

Secondly, elevation of soul may also be brought about as ollows: "An ever-increasing, admiring love frequently brings to ie mind such floods of Divine Light and overwhelms the soul vith such a realisation of the Divine Loveliness that she ecomes bewildered. Struck to her very foundations she loses old of the body. Just as the deeper a streak of lightning strikes ie quicker it mounts, so is it with the soul in the condition just described. The more such a soul discounts herself and sinks in self-abasement at the presence of God's most admirable loveliness, so much the higher and quicker does she rise. The greater the ardour of her loving, admiring desires, the higher does she ascend. She is carried out of herself until she is elevated even to the topmost heights" (Richard of St. Victor.) There, like another Esther, she bursts forth into a paean of praise. "I saw Thee, My Lord," she exclaims, "as an Angel of God; and my heart was troubled for fear of Thy Majesty, for Thou, My Lord, art very admirable; and Thy Face is full of graces" (Esth. xv, 16, 17.)

Finally, a similar transport occurs when exceeding, exulting joy takes possession of the soul. "When the soul has drunk of an abundance of interior sweetness and is completely inebriated with delight, she forgets altogether what she is and what she was. There and then she is transformed. She is thrown into a state of supernatural love, and is rapt into a marvelous, bliss-producing ecstasy" (Richard of St. Victor.) With the Psalmist in transport she sings: "How lovely are Thy tabernacles, O Lord of Hosts. My soul longs and faints for the courts of the Lord. My heart and my flesh have rejoiced in the living God" (Ps. lxxxiii, 23.)

Thus is it that the servant of God should train herself in the practice of fervent prayer. Frequent prayer, the frequent use of prayer will teach her and render her fit to contemplate things divine. The eye of a heart purified and washed by prayer can see the things above. Purified by frequent prayer the soul comes to taste and to enjoy the sweets of God.

It is not becoming for a soul fashioned after and stamped with God's image to fritter away her time busying herself with earthly cares. A soul redeemed by Christ's Precious Blood and made for eternal happiness ought "to ascend even above the Cherubim and fly upon the wings of the wind" (Cf. Ps. xvii, ii), hat is, the wings of the Angels. She ought to ascend high and ontemplate the Most Holy Trinity and Christ's Sacred Humanity. She should meditate on the glory of the citizens of he city above, and ponder on the happiness of the Angels and Saints.

Tell me, who today explores into the regions of heavenly glory? Who are they that in heart and soul pass their time thinking on he things above? They are the few. We may today with truth ay even of many religious what St. Bernard said: "Many who hould have been devoutly penetrating the heavens, viewing here the many mansions, holding converse with the apostles and the prophets and assisting in wonder at the triumphs of the martyrs, instead find themselves as base slaves to the body, erving the flesh and pampering its gluttonous desires" (S. Bern. Serm. xxxv on the Canticle of Cant., 3.)

CHAPTER VI: THE REMEMBRANCE OF CHRIST'S PASSION

Christ's death on the Cross should live in our thoughts and imagination, for frequent thought on the Passion of Christ keeps aflame and brings to intense heat the fires of earnest piety. We must picture to the eyes of our heart Christ dying on the Cross if we would prevent the fires of devotion within us burning themselves out. An apposite quotation bears this out: "The fire on my altar shall always burn, and the priest shall feed it, putting wood on it every day" (Levit. Vi, 12.)

Let me explain, most devout Mother. The altar of God is your heart. On the altar of your heart the fire of intense heat must burn constantly. You must feed the fire each day with the wood of the cross and the remembrance of the Passion of Christ. Isaiah, the prophet, preaches a similar truth: "You shall draw waters with joy out of the Saviour's fountains" (Is. xii, 3.) In other words, if the grace of tears, the tears of thanksgiving, the tears of fervent piety are sought, such tears must be drawn from the Saviour's fountains—that is, from the five wounds of Jesus Christ.

Draw near, O handmaid, with loving steps to Jesus wounded for you, to Jesus crowned with thorns, to Jesus nailed to the gibbet of the Cross. With the Blessed Apostle St. Thomas, so not merely gaze on the print of the nails in Christ's hands; be not satisfied with putting your finger into the holes made by the nails in His hands; neither let it be sufficient even to put your hand into the wound in His side (Cf. John xx, 25, 27.) But enter bodily by the door in His side and go straight up to the very Heart of Jesus. There, burning with love for Christ Crucified, be transformed into Christ.

Fastened to the Cross by the nails of the fear of God, transfixed by the lance of the love of your inmost heart, pierced through and through by the sword of the most tender compassion, seek

›r nothing else, wish for nothing else, look for consolation in othing else except in dying with Christ on the Cross. Then, at ıst, will you cry out with Paul the Apostle: "I have been crucified ith Christ. I live, now not I; but Christ liveth in me" (Gal. ii, 19, 0.)

/hen you meditate on the passion of Christ proceed as follows: hink how Christ's sufferings were the most disgraceful, the ıost bitter, the most complete, and the most protracted.

ı the first place, O worthy handmaid of God, dwell on the fact ıat the death of Jesus Christ, your Spouse, was the most isgraceful possible. I say the most disgraceful because he was rucified as a thief and a highway robber. The old Law reserved ıe punishment of death by crucifixion for the villainous among ıieves and the utterly criminal among robbers (Cf. Num. xxv, 4; eut. xxi, 22 sq.; II Kings xxi, 6–9; Esth. vii, 10 and ix, 13; also ial. iii, 13.)

.eflect for a moment, and realise how Christ suffered greater isgrace than usually befell a criminal. He was crucified on lount Calvary, a place disgusting and vile because of its ssociations (Matt xxvii, 33; Mark xv, 22; Luke xxiii, 33; John ix, 17; and cf. S. Bonav. on Wisd. ii 19 etc., Com. on John xix, 7; Luke xxiii, 33.) It was a heap of dead men's bodies and ones, and was the spot given over to the execution of those ondemned to death for murderous deeds. There only vile riminals were beheaded; only vile criminals were hanged or rucified.

. little more thought will enable you to realize still better the reater disgrace that was meted out to Christ. He was hanged s a robber among robbers. He was placed in the midst of obbers as the Chief, the Prince, the King of robbers. Hence we nd Isaiah saying: "He was reputed with the wicked" (Is. liii, 12;

cf. also Matt, xxvii. 38; Mark xv, 27; Luke xxii, 37; xxiii, 33; John xix, 18.)

Consider even a little longer how greatly disgraced was your Spouse. As though He were unfit to live or die upon the earth, He was raised into the air and was hanged between heaven an earth. O worthy indignity! O fitting injury! The earth is refused to the Lord of the earth. Nothing in the world is considered viler than the Lord of the world. His condemnation was an insult; to crucify Him was still worse. “He was numbered and condemned among the wicked” (Isa liii, 12.) To compel Him to die shoulder to shoulder with criminals increased His shame. Lastly they put Him to death on the vile hill of Calvary and thus intensified His shame beyond understanding. Christ suffered the very extremit of insult and unparalleled disgrace.

O good Jesus, O kind Saviour, not once but often wert Thou outraged. When a man is repeatedly put to shame, his shame is thereby increased. Alas! they heaped insult upon insult on Thee They bound thee, O Lord Jesus, with ropes in the Garden. In the house of Annas they slapped Thy face. They spat upon Thee when Thou wast in the hall of Caiaphas. They made sport and mockery of Thee in the presence of Herod. They forced Thee to carry the Cross along the road, and on Golgotha they crucified Thee. Alas, alas! The Freedom of the Captives is enslaved, the Glory of the Angels is mocked, the Life of Men is done to death! O you wretched men, you said: “Let us condemn Him to a most shameful death” (Wisd. ii, 20.) What you said you would do, you have done, and done well!

Realizing it all, St. Bernard cries out, “He emptied Himself taking the form of a servant *[Phil, ii, 7.]* He was a Son and He became a servant, but for Him it was insufficient to be a mere servant and to live in subjection. He took to Himself the form of a wicked servant, thus making Himself an object for the scourge and fitting Himself to pay the penalties for crimes He had never ommitted" (S. Bern. Holy Week Serm. 10.) He was not merely ne Servant of the servants of God, as is the Pope, but He ecame the Servant even of the servants of the evil one; for did le not forgive and cleanse His executioners from the guilt of the oul crimes they had committed? This did not suffice. Lest you hould dread the prospect of suffering similarly, He chose a eath more humiliating and more confusing than any other. "He umbled Himself, becoming obedient unto death, even to the eath of the Cross" (Phil, ii, 8.) What else could have reduced lim so to nothingness?

ome now, O virgin devoted to God, and consider attentively ne bitter cruelty of Christ's sufferings. When harassed and earied with pain, a man ordinarily finds some relief and omfort by contracting his limbs and muscles. With His hands nd legs extended on the cross, movement was impossible for hrist and so such relaxation was denied Him. Worn out with ufferings, He did not find even the least ease or lessening of ain. There was no place whereon He might rest His Divine dorable head as His soul was about to take her flight.

et us go into the matter of Christ's bitter sufferings more losely. The more tender a body, the more acutely does it suffer Cf. S. Bonav. III Sent. d. xvi, I, qu. 2.) A woman's body is more ender than a man's. There was never flesh more adapted for uffering than the virginal flesh of Christ. It was born of a Virgin, ho conceived of the Holy Ghost, and the Man Christ was the enderest of virgins. It was possible for Christ to suffer the most xcruciating sufferings of all.

ctually, at the mere thought of the death that over-shadowed lim, "His soul became sad," and as the sadness reverberated His tender flesh, "the sweat" of his Body oozed out in thick rops "as a sweat of blood dripping to the ground" (Matt, xxvi, 8; Luke xxii, 44.) What must have been the anguish and torture le endured during the course of His Passion! St. Bernard says:

"O Jesus Christ, the blood which You sweated from Your sacred body, and which flowed to the ground as You prayed, most surely showed the anguish of Your heart" (S. Bern., Serm. on the Life and Pass. of the Lord, 6.)

"O sweetest Child," cried out St. Anselm, "what did You do that You should be treated so? O most Lovable of Youths, what was Your sin that Your judgment should be so severe? Alas, I am the cause of Your grief, I inflicted the deadly blow!" (S. Anselm, Prayer.)

Once again, exercise your attention and come to a better understanding of Christ's bitterly cruel death. When a person is innocent of a crime, the more innocent he is, the more poignantly does he feel the punishment inflicted. If Christ had endured the tortures of His passion because of His own sins, His sufferings would have been somewhat tolerable. But "He did no sin, neither was guile found in his mouth" (I Pet. ii, 22.) Pilate bore witness to this: "I find no cause of death in Him" (Cf. John xviii, 38.) So too testifies the seventh chapter of the Book of Wisdom: He is "the brightness of eternal light, and the unspotted mirror of God's majesty, and the image of His goodness" (Wisd. vii, 26.)

Consider still further how painful was the death of your beloved Spouse, Jesus Christ. Suffering is bad enough, but when every torture conceivable is inflicted, what could be more painful? Christ, your Spouse, suffered in every part of His body so that no member, not even the least, escaped its own particular suffering. No part of His body was too small or too trivial but that it had its full share of torture. "From the sole of His foot unto the crown of His head was no soundness in Him" (Cf. Is. i, 6.)

Hence, overwhelmed with the prophetic vision of Christ's too great sufferings, Jeremiah puts the following words into the Saviour's mouth: "Oh, all ye who pass by the way, look and see there be any sorrow like unto My sorrow" (Lamentations, i, 2.) In very deed, my Lord Jesus Christ, there was never grief ke Your grief, no sorrow like Your sorrow, no suffering omparable with Your suffering. You shed Your blood so rofusely that Your body was bathed in blood.

) good Jesus, O sweetest Jesus! Not merely drops of blood, ut rivers of blood flowed liberally from Your five wounds when 'our body was hanging nailed to the cross! Blood flowed in orrents from Your head when you were crowned with thorns! 3lood flowed from the whole of Your body whilst You were eing scourged with the lash! Blood flowed from Your heart vhen You were pierced with the lance! If any blood remained in 'ou, it could have been only by a miracle! Tell me, oh, tell me,) sweet Lord, why did You shed so much blood? Why did you hed all the blood of Your body? One drop of Your sacred recious blood would have sufficed for the world's redemption. Vhy did you do it?

know, O Lord, why. It was simply and solely to show how much 'ou love me.

What return, then, shall I make to the Lord for all that He has lone for me?" (Ps. cxv, 12) Most surely, my Lord, as long as I ive I shall never forget how Thou spentest Thyself in my behalf. shall bear constantly in mind Thy preaching, the weariness caused Thee by Thy travelling up and down the country, Thy vigils and prayers, Thy compassionate tears, Thy griefs, the nsults that were heaped upon Thee, the spittle and the sneers, he blows, the nails and wounds. Otherwise, were I to forget hese things, rightly would the blood of this Just Man, which was shed upon the earth, be required of me" (S. Bern. Holy Week Serm. ii; cf. Matt, xxii, 35.)

Who therefore, will give water to my head, and a fountain of ears to my eyes," (Jer. ix, i), that day and night I may weep for the death of my Lord Jesus Christ? He suffered death not because of His own sins, but because of mine. In the words of Isaiah, "He was wounded for our iniquities, He was bruised for our sins" (Is. liii, 5.)

Lastly, ponder attentively and carefully on the protracted duration of Christ's sufferings and death. Christ carried around with Him His sufferings from the beginning to the end. From the first moment of His birth to the last flicker of His life, His death and passion were ever present to His mind. The Psalmist assures us of this fact: "I am poor, and in labours from My youth" (Ps. lxxxvii, 16.) The same thought is expressed elsewhere: "I have been scourged all the day" (Ps. lxxii, 14.) That is, I have been scourged during the whole of my life.

A further thought is suggested for reflection. The arrangements made for inflicting Christ's sufferings were peculiar to His passion. Everything was done to protract the torture. He was suspended in the air that consciousness should endure and thus He would remain in pain to the end. Further, everything tended to keep Him alive, and thus the torture of a lingering death was His. Death by crucifixion kept Him conscious and in agony to the last moment.

From all that I have said, dear spouse of Christ and servant of God, you will gather a clear idea of Christ's sufferings and death. You will be able to realize somewhat how the sacred passion induced in our Lord a sense of unutterable disgrace. His sufferings were cruelly painful, and they extended to every member of His body and to every faculty of His soul. In a word, Christ's sufferings and death were unique in their kind and protracted in their duration.

Christ accepted these sufferings and death to gain your devoted love. Through thought on these sufferings and out of gratitude, He wishes you to love Him. He desires you to love Him with your whole heart, with your whole mind, and with your whole soul (Cf. Matt, xxii, 37.) To save a slave He became a slave. What could prove better His kindness of heart? What better incentive to enable us to work for our own salvation could He give than His own example? To appease the divine anger He accepted the death that the justice of God demanded and thereby gave us an example of obedience.

Could you name a better inducement to love God than this love that the Son of God has shown for you? In spite of our worthlessness, though we deserve punishment, He "laid down His life" (Cf. John x, 15) for us. His kindness reached such depths and such heights that it is impossible to imagine anything more tender, more kind or more lovable. The greatness of His love becomes more evident the more we realize the abject and terrible nature of Christ's sufferings. For God "spared not even His own Son, but delivered Him up for us all; how hath He not also, with Him, given us all things?" (Rom. viii, 32.) This is the way God has loved us, and has invited us to love Him and to imitate Him in His love for us.

Woe, therefore, to those who are ungrateful for the benefits accruing to them from this great kindness of Christ! Woe to those in whose souls the death of Christ produces no good effects! "Look," says St. Bernard, "at Christ on the Cross! Look at Him, His head bent down as though He longed to stoop to kiss us! Look at Him, His arms extended to take us in a loving embrace! Look at His hands so deeply pierced to pour out riches for our benefit. Look at His sacred side opened wide to permit the love of His heart to reach us! Look at Him, His whole body extended to give Himself entirely to us! Woe to those, I say it a second time, who by their sins 'crucify again to themselves the Son of God' *[Heb. vi, 6,]* and have added to the grief of His wounds." (Ps. lxviii, 27.)

Woe, further, to those whose hearts will not soften nor give way to grief at the thought of Christ s sufferings. Woe to those whom the shedding of God's blood in such abundance and the payment of such a great price cannot warm and inflame to the practice of virtue, kind charity and good works! Certainly, such people are "the enemies of the cross of Christ" (Phil, iii, 18.) On a day long since past, onlookers blasphemed Christ hanging on the Cross. Sinners do worse. They blaspheme Christ the Son of God sitting at the right hand of His Father in Heaven.

Speaking through the mouth of His servant St. Bernard, Our Lord complains of these ungrateful ones and rebukes them. "Man," He says, "look what I suffer for you. What grief is there such as I suffer? In the act of dying for you I appeal to you. Look at the sufferings heaped upon Me. Look at the nails which dig into My flesh. You can see the exterior suffering, but My interior grief of heart is greater still when I realise that in spite of all you remain so ungrateful" (S. Bern. III Sent. d. 16.)

Take care, Mother, lest you be wanting in gratitude for such benefits. A great price has been paid for you. Have a care lest you be lacking in devotion or show too little attachment to Christ. Place Jesus Christ "as a seal on your heart" (Cf. Cant, viii, 6.) Just as a seal is impressed upon soft wax, impress your Spouse Jesus Christ on your heart. Say to Him with the Prophet: "My heart is become like melting wax" (Ps. xxi, 15.) Put Him "as a seal upon thy arm" (Cf. Cant, viii, 6) so that you may never cease doing good and may never tire of working for the honour of the name of your Lord Jesus Christ. When you have done everything, when you have spent yourself in His service, begin afresh, as though you had never done anything for Him.

If ever anything sad befalls you, or anything grieves you, or if perchance something causes you weariness or bitterness of heart, or sweetness of soul turns insipid, lift up immediately your eyes to your Lord hanging nailed to the Cross. Look upon Him, is head crowned with thorns! Gaze upon the nails, the iron ails which fasten Him to the Cross, and upon the lance piercing is sacred side. In all trying moments, picture and contemplate ıe wounds in His hands and feet, picture to yourself the 'ounds in His most blessed head, the wound in His sacred de, the wounds of His whole body. Call to mind that He was 'ounded for your sake, that he suffered for you and that His ufferings were so great because He loved you beyond ompare.

elieve me, a glance at such pictures and thought on such ufferings will quickly change your sadness into joy. What was eavy to bear will become light. What causes your weariness ill become something to love. The rugged and the difficult will e changed into sweetness and relish, so that soon, with Holy ob, you will begin to exclaim: "The things which before my soul 'ould not touch," now when I look upon the "anguish" of Christ ıre my meats" (Job vi, 7.) It is as though you were to say: The ood things which were distasteful to my soul are now become ırough the passion of Christ, which I realise, sweet and savory.

ı the Chronicles of the Franciscan Order there is related the ıllowing story (Cf. Chronicles xxiv, 3): A certain man being onverted and having entered the Order eventually became npatient with the frugality of the Friars. The discipline of the riary, too, upset him. Once, being very perturbed and lost to all atience on account of these things, he threw himself down efore a crucifix. With bitter tears he enumerated the intolerable ardships he was called upon to endure: the burdens of the eligious life, the scant and frugal fare, the tastelessness of the ood and drink. While he poured forth his grievances, suddenly lood began to ooze from the side of the image of Christ nailed ı the cross. As he continued his weeping and wailing, the leeding image of the crucified Christ spoke to him these words: Vhen you find your food or drink distasteful, dip it into the auce of the blood of Christ."

CHAPTER VII: THE PERFECT LOVE OF GOD

Earlier on, guided by the Holy Spirit, I explained to you how you should train your faculties so that passing from "virtue to virtue" (Ps. lxxxiii, 8), you might advance step by step in the way of holiness. I come now to the soul or the life-giving principle of all the virtues. I refer to charity, the virtue alone capable of leading a man to real holiness. In mortifying the flesh, in overcoming sin and in attaining to grace, nothing avails like charity. Would you reach the highest rung of the ladder of perfection? Nothing could possibly be devised to help you more than charity.

In his book on the contemplative life Prosper writes: "Charity is the life of virtue and the death of vice" (Prosper iii, 13.) "As wax melts before the fire so" vices "vanish into nothingnesss" when they come "face to face" with charity (Cf. Ps. lxvii, 3.) Charity is a virtue of such power that it can both close the gates of hell and open wide the portals of eternal bliss. Charity provides the hope of salvation and alone renders us lovable in God's sight. It is so great a virtue that among the virtues it is called the virtue. To be founded and rooted in charity is to be wealthy and happy, for without charity we are indigent and wretched (Cf. Apoc. iii, 17.)

Commenting on the words of St. Paul (I Cor. xiii, 2), "If I have not charity," Peter Lombard quoting St. Augustine says: "Just think a moment on the excellence of charity. Without charity it is useless to possess all else; possess it, and you have everything. To begin to possess it is to possess the Holy Ghost" (Peter Lomb. Comm. on I Cor., quoting S. Aug.) Elsewhere St. Augustine says: "If it is the practice of virtue which leads to Heaven, I unhesitatingly affirm that the virtue to be practised is the pure love of God" (S. Aug. De Morib. Ecc., I, xv, 25.)

Since it is a virtue of supreme importance, charity must be insisted on before all else. Let it be well noted, however, that the harity leading to the possession of God is not any charity, but olely the charity, the love that loves God above all things and ›ves God's creatures for God's sake.

'he Holy Gospel gives a clear lead on the qualities of this love ›r God. "Thou shalt love the Lord Thy God with thy whole heart, nd with thy whole soul, and with thy whole mind" (Matt, xxii, 37; lark xii, 30; Luke x, 27.) Think well, most cherished handmaid f Jesus Christ, on the love which your Beloved Jesus demands om you. He, your Best Beloved, wishes you to love, and to ›ve Him most lovingly. He desires that you give yourself body nd soul, mind and heart entirely to love for Him. He wishes to hare your love with no one else. He commands that you be all lis.

low is this to be done? What are you to do so that there can be o doubt that you love the Lord God with your whole heart? low is the love of the whole heart given?

'or answer, let me quote St. John Chrysostom: "To love God vith your whole heart it is required that nothing attract your eart more than God attracts it. You must not take more leasure in the things of earth than in God. Honours and places f position, love of father and mother and relatives must not ount in the scale of love before love of God. Be it friend or elative, place or position, be it what it may, if anything takes up our heart's love more than God, you do not love God with your vhole heart." (S. Chrys., Hom. on Matt.)

beg you, dear handmaid of Christ, not to deceive yourself bout your love. If you love anything which is not in God, or if oving you do not love for God's sake, you do not yet love God vith your whole heart. It is on this account that St. Augustine vrites: "O Lord, whoever divides his love with You and anything ›r anyone else, gives You less love than is Your due" (S. Aug. Conf. xxix, 40.) If your love for anything does not lead you to greater love for God, you do not yet love Him with your whole heart. If for the love of anything dear to you, you neglect to give Christ those things that are His by right, again I say, you do not love Him with your whole heart.

We must love Our Lord Jesus Christ not only with all our heart, but also with all our soul. The same blessed St. Augustine explains how this is to be done. "To love God with one's whole soul, is so to center the will on loving Him that nothing in any way opposed to Him wins the least of our love. For the soul to give in its entirety all the love of which its faculties are capable, she must willingly, without the least reluctance or reserve, give her love in full accord with all Her Lord's desires" (S. Aug. Serm cviii, 35.)

To love Him because it pleases you to give him your love, or because the world recommends, or the flesh suggests, such love, is not the love God asks. If for the love of Jesus Christ you would be prepared gallantly and lovingly to die in His service should occasion arise, then most certainly you do love Him with your whole soul. If you do not love Him for His own sake or would find it difficult to die for His sake, your love is imperfect. It is not the love of your whole soul that you offer Him. Conform your will in all things to the Divine Will. This is what God demands. Do this, and the love wherewith you love God will be the love of your whole soul.

Not only must you love your Spouse, Jesus Christ, with your whole heart and soul, you must also love Him with your whole mind. What "with your whole mind" means, St. Augustine explains: "To love God with all the love of which the mind is capable is to love Him unceasingly. It means that He must neve be absent from our loving thoughts. Memory must keep Him constantly in mind" (S. Aug. Serm. cviii.)

:HAPTER VIII: FINAL PERSEVERANCE

is not enough to be virtuous. To be firmly rooted in virtue, to ossess virtuous habits, does not render us glorious in God's ight. Something else is still wanting. To be an object of glory to e eye of God we must possess the culminating virtue, the rown and consummation of all virtues: perseverance. No ortal being whatever, no matter how perfect He may seem, hould be praised while he is still living. Let a man be praised ot because he has begun a good work but because he has rought it to a good and happy completion. "Perseverance is the nd, acme and crown of the virtues. It nurtures and fits one for erit; it leads to and culminates in reward" (S. Bern. Ep. cxxix, .)

lence St. Bernard says, "Take away perseverance and nothing emains. For the fulfilment of duty, the performance of good leeds and the exercise of fortitude will not procure the grace ufficient to obtain eternal praise" (Ibid.) It will avail a man little o have been a religious, to have been patient and humble, levout and chaste, to have loved God and to have exercised imself in all the virtues, if he continues not to the end. He must ersevere to win the crown. In the race of the spiritual life all the irtues run, but only perseverance "receives the prize" (1 Cor. ix, 4.) It is not the beginner in virtue but "he that shall persevere nto the end that shall be saved" (Matt. x, 22.) "What is the use f seeds sprouting if afterwards they wither and die?" asks St. hrysostom (S. Chrys., Hom. xxxiii, 5.) None whatever!

f then, dear spouse of Jesus Christ, your virtues are productive f good works—and I assume that this is so—be sure to ontinue in your good practices. Persevere in your virtuous abits. Make it a practice ever and constantly to increase in the erformance of good works. Wage the war of Christ with all your night. Practise and increase in virtue up to the very moment of leath. Then, when your last moment comes and your life is brought to a close, God will give you the crown of honour and glory as the prize and reward of your labour.

Your Best Beloved Lord Jesus Christ has assured you of this. These are His words, written for your instruction by the inspired author of the Apocalypse: "Be thou faithful unto death, and I will give thee the crown of life" (Apoc. ii, 10.) What is this crown if not the reward of eternal life? The heart of every Christian ought to burn with the desire of winning this reward. In value there is nothing comparable to it; it is priceless. It surpasses the mathematician's power, says St. Gregory, to count its varying parts and manifold possibilities (Cf. S. Greg. II Hom. on Gospels xxxvii, I.) There is no limit to its duration. It is to be enjoyed eternally. It can never cease.

Your Beloved Spouse Jesus Christ invites you to win this prize, to gain this crown. Listen to what He says to you in the Canticle of Canticles: "Come from Libanus, my Spouse, come my friend from Libanus, come and thou shalt be crowned" (Cant, iv, 8.) "Arise at once," you who call yourself "the friend" of God, the spouse of Jesus Christ, the best beloved of the Eternal King, "come, make haste" (Cant, ii, 10) to the marriage feast of the Son of God (Cf. Apoc. xix, 9.) "Everything is prepared" (Matt, xxii, 4); the whole court of Heaven awaits you (Cf. S. Bonav. Soliloq.)

Three wonderful joys are prepared for you in the heavenly Kingdom. First, there is a servant of noble lineage, beautiful to look upon, who will be at your beck and call. Second, there is a food of priceless worth and alluring in its sweetness to refresh you. Third, there is a society, sweet and delightful and lovable beyond conception. Such fellowship will intensify your joy.

Arise then and speed with haste to the nuptials, because of the transcendent beauty of the servant who waits to perform your commands. That servant is not one only, for the whole angelic ssembly—yes, even the very Son of God will be in readiness attend to your wants. Listen to what He says of Himself as eported in the Holy Gospel of St. Luke: “Amen, I say to you, at He will gird Himself, and make them sit down at table, and assing, will minister unto them” (Luke xii, 37; Cf. S. Bonav. oliloq. iv, 12.) Ah, then, indeed great will be the glory of the oor and lowly, to have the Son of God, the Eternal King inistering to their wants and the whole court of Heaven iligently obeying their behests.

precious, delight-giving food, a food to refresh you, awaits you ere. The very Son of God with His own hands will prepare the able. He pledged His word to this, as we read in St. Luke: “I ispose to you, as my Father has disposed to me a Kingdom; at you may eat and drink at my table, in my Kingdom” (Luke xii, 29 & 30.) Oh, how sweet and luscious is that food which od in all His sweetness has prepared for the poor! (Cf. Ps. vii, ii.) Oh, how blessed will he be who eats that food in the ingdom of Heaven! In the precincts of the virginal womb of lary that food was prepared by the burning love of the Holy host. “If any man eats of this Bread he shall live forever” (John i, 52.)

Vith such food, with such bread the King of Heaven feeds and efreshes His chosen ones. This we are told also in the book of Visdom. “Thou didst feed Thy people with the food of Angels nd gavest them bread from Heaven, prepared without labour, aving in it all that is delicious and the sweetness of every taste, nd serving every man’s will” (Wisd. xvi, 20, 21.) Such, in a vord, is the repast provided at the heavenly table.

here is also a loving and exceedingly lovable fellowship repared, that your happiness in Heaven may be complete. here the company will be the Father, Jesus, and the Holy pirit, together with Mary and her throng of chaste virgins. here you will dwell with the Apostles, the Martyrs, the

Confessors, the whole army of the elect. How altogether miserable it will be for those who fail to be associated with this most noble band! If there is one who does not long to have part in this fellowship, all desire in him must be dead.

You, O most noble handmaid of Christ, I know, desire Christ. You are striving to gain possession of Christ and you are striving with all your might. Your great desire is to languish in the companionship and embraces of the Eternal King.

“Well now, have courage, inflame your heart, arouse your soul, keep your intellect on the alert and think well on what you are able to do. If each good thing separately may furnish delight, reflect how replete with delight must be the good that contains all the delight which all good things can produce collectively. If the life of the creature is good, what goodness must there be in the Creator of life? If the health of the body is an inestimable delight, what is to be said of that Health, that saving Power which is the Author of all health and salvation, whether of soul or body?

“When one possesses this great Good there is no limit to one’s possessions. There is nothing that does not belong to him. Whatever he desires will be his. Whatever he does not want he will not have. In Heaven, undoubtedly, will be found the good things of soul and body—good things such as ‘eye hath not seen, nor ear heard, and that have neither entered into the heart of man’ *[I Cor. ii, 9.]* Why then do you wander about so much, searching for good things for soul and body? Love the One Only Good. Love the Good in which all other good is contained. That One Good suffices. Long for that Goodness alone which is all that is Good. It is all that you need” (S. Anselm, Proslog. xxiv & xxvi.)

n Heaven, Mother dear, all that you love, all that you desire is ɔ be found. What is it you love? O loving virgin, on what do you enter all the desires of your heart?

s it beauty which charms you and claims your love? If so, In leaven 'the just shall shine as the sun' *[Matt. xiii, 43.]*

f a long life, a life full of health is what you mostly wish, in leaven you will realize your desire, for there the righteous shall ve forever. 'The salvation of the just is for evermore' *[Wisd. v, 6; Ps. xxxvi, 39.]*

s it a complete, a total satisfaction that you crave? If so, 'there ıey will be satisfied when the glory of God shall appear' *[Cf. Ps. vi, 15.]*

Would you be inebriated, intoxicated with delight? 'They shall e inebriated with the plenty of the house of God' *[Cf. Ps. xxxv, .]*

Do you look to be delighted with sweet melody? Well, in leaven the Angelic Choirs chant in harmony praising God vithout ceasing.

s it in loving friendship you seek your delight? In Heaven the aints love God more than themselves. So, too, they love each ther more than themselves and God loves them infinitely more han they love themselves.

Should it be peace of heart and union which appeal to you, ealise that in Heaven there is no will but the Will of God.

If honour and riches please you, God 'will place' His servants nd his handmaids 'over many things' *[Matt, xxv, 21.]* 215 They shall be called,' and will be indeed, 'the sons and daughters, he children of God' *[Matt, v, 9.]* Where God is there they also shall be who are 'the heirs indeed of God, and co-heirs with Christ' *[Cf. John xii, 26 and Rom. viii, 17.]*' (S. Anselm, Proslog xxv.)

"Where goodness to such a degree and to such an excess exists, what will be the qualities and extent of the joy there to b found? Certainly, O Lord Jesus, 'eye hath not seen, nor ear heard, neither in this life hath it entered into the heart of man' *[I Cor ii, 9]* to conceive how Thy Blessed ones will love Thee and rejoice on Thy account when they revel in heavenly bliss" (S. Anselm, Proslog. xxvi.)

Whatever measure men set for their love of God here will be th measure of their rejoicing with God in Heaven. Therefore love God intensely here, and your rejoicing will be intense hereafter. Continue to grow in the love of God here, and afterwards in Heaven you will possess the fullness of eternal joy. "Ponder in mind on the joy of Heaven, talk it over with yourself, love it with all your heart and speak of it to others. Let your soul hunger an your body thirst for it. Long for it with all your being until at last you 'enter into the joy of your Lord' *[Matt. xxv, 21.]*' (S. Anselm, ibid.)

Sigh for it until you fall into the loving embrace of your Spouse and are introduced by Him into His own bridal chamber, where with the Father and the Holy Spirit He lives and reigns, One God, for ever and ever. AMEN.

Made in the USA
Columbia, SC
06 February 2021

32449662R00039